The Early
RETIREMENT
BLUEPRINT

Achieving Financial Independence and Retiring Early

JEFFREY FERON

TABLE OF CONTENT

INTRODUCTION

Welcome to "The Early Retirement Blueprint: Achieving Financial Independence and Retiring Early". In this book, we will explore the journey towards early retirement and provide you with the necessary guidance to make it a reality.

Retiring early is not just about escaping the nine-to-five grind; it's about gaining financial independence, pursuing your passions, and living life on your terms. Whether you dream of traveling the world, starting a new business, or simply having more time for family and hobbies, early retirement can be your ticket to a fulfilling and purposeful life.

In each chapter, we will delve into different aspects of early retirement, from building a solid financial foundation to investing wisely, creating multiple streams of income, and designing your ideal retirement lifestyle. We will also address the challenges and obstacles that may arise along the way and provide strategies to overcome them.

So, if you're ready to take control of your financial future, gain freedom from the daily grind, and embark on a life of early retirement, this book is your roadmap. Let's begin the journey towards financial independence and a fulfilling retirement on your terms.

"The early retirement blueprint isn't just about financial independence; it's a roadmap to reclaiming your time and freedom."

1

THE ROADMAP TO EARLY RETIREMENT

Retiring early may seem like an unattainable dream, but with careful planning and disciplined execution, it can become a reality. In this chapter, we will lay the groundwork for your early retirement journey.

First and foremost, it's essential to understand the concept of early retirement. Unlike traditional retirement, which often occurs in your 60s or later, early retirement allows you to leave the workforce and enjoy financial freedom at a younger age. It gives you the opportunity to pursue your passions, spend more time with loved ones, and live life on your own terms.

To embark on this journey, you need to set clear financial goals and create a timeline for achieving them. Begin by assessing your current financial situation, including your assets, and liabilities, income, and expenses. This will give you a realistic picture of where you stand and what steps you need to take to reach your retirement goals.

Next, you'll need to develop a budget and track your expenses meticulously. By understanding your spending habits and identifying areas where you can cut back, you can increase your savings rate and accelerate your path to early retirement. Remember, every dollar saved today is an investment in your future freedom.

In addition to saving, you'll also need to focus on increasing your income. Explore strategies for boosting your earning potential, such as negotiating a higher salary, pursuing promotions, or even taking on a side hustle. The more money you can earn, the faster you can save and invest towards your early retirement goal.

Speaking of investing, it's crucial to educate yourself on different investment vehicles and develop a sound investment strategy. Diversify your portfolio to spread risk and maximize returns. Consider long-term growth investments like stocks and index funds, as well as more stable options like bonds and real estate.

Lastly, remember that early retirement is not just about the financial aspect. It's also about finding fulfillment and purpose beyond work. Start exploring your passions and interests, and think about how you can incorporate them into your post-retirement life. Whether it's traveling,

> *"Achieving financial independence and retiring early requires a mindset of discipline, determination, and delayed gratification."*

2

BUILDING A SOLID FINANCIAL FOUNDATION

Embarking on the path to early retirement demands the construction of a formidable financial foundation. This chapter serves as a compass, directing you through the essential steps required to forge a resilient financial base.

Assessing Your Current Financial Situation

Before laying the groundwork for financial freedom, it is imperative to comprehend your current financial standing. Conduct a thorough examination of your income, expenditures, assets, and liabilities. Derive your net worth by deducting liabilities from assets to gain a crystal-clear view of your financial well-being and pinpoint areas that warrant enhancement.

Developing a Budget and Tracking Expenses

The creation of a budget stands as a pivotal stride in the effective management of finances. Initiate the process by itemizing all revenue streams and categorizing expenditures comprehensively, encompassing both fixed and variable costs. Monitor your spending over a few months to acquire a realistic perspective on your financial outflows.

Once armed with a thorough comprehension of your income and outlays, construct a budget aligned with your financial aspirations. Allocate a segment of your earnings towards savings and investments, identifying potential expense cutbacks to bolster your savings rate.

Strategies for Debt Management and Elimination

The specter of debt can impede progress towards early retirement. Developing a strategy to navigate and eradicate debt is paramount. Catalog all debts, including credit card balances, student loans, and mortgages. Prioritize settling high-interest debts while adhering to minimum payments on others.

Explore avenues like debt consolidation or refinancing to mitigate interest rates and streamline debt repayment. Delve into strategies such as the debt snowball or debt avalanche method to expedite debt clearance. The elimination of debt frees up additional resources for saving and investing towards early retirement objectives.

Building an Emergency Fund

An emergency fund stands as a vital component of a robust financial foundation, acting as a safety net against unforeseen expenses or financial setbacks. Endeavor to accumulate three to six months' worth of living expenses in your emergency fund.

Commence by establishing a realistic savings target and regularly contributing to your emergency fund. Automating your savings facilitates consistent fund growth. Maintain your emergency fund in a separate account—accessible but not too tempting for non-emergency expenses.

Developing a Long-Term Savings and Investment Strategy

Realizing early retirement necessitates prudent money management through astute saving and investing. Develop a comprehensive long-term savings and investment strategy aligned with your goals and risk tolerance. Seeking guidance from a financial advisor can aid in crafting a personalized plan.

Maximize contributions to retirement accounts, such as a 401(k) or IRA, and leverage employer matching contributions for an added savings boost. Explore alternative investment avenues like taxable brokerage accounts or real estate to diversify your portfolio.

Regularly reassess and adjust your investment strategy as circumstances dictate. Stay abreast of market trends, seizing opportunities to optimize returns. Bear in mind, achieving early retirement demands disciplined savings and judicious investment decisions.

By fortifying a robust financial foundation, you pave the way for a successful journey towards early retirement. Evaluate your current financial landscape, formulate a budget, manage and eliminate debt, cultivate an emergency fund, and devise a long-term savings and investment strategy. Armed with a resilient foundation, you'll be well-positioned to realize your early retirement aspirations.

"The key to the early retirement blueprint lies in living below your means, investing wisely, and valuing experiences over possessions."

3

MAXIMIZING INCOME AND SAVINGS

In your journey towards early retirement, maximizing your income and savings is crucial. This chapter will explore strategies to increase your earning potential and optimize your savings rate.

Strategies for Increasing Your Income

To accelerate your path to early retirement, consider various strategies to boost your income. One option is to negotiate a higher salary or seek promotions at your current job. Highlight your accomplishments, skills, and the value you bring to the organization. Additionally, invest in your professional development to enhance your qualifications and increase your marketability.

Another avenue to explore is the world of side hustles and freelancing. Leverage your skills and interests to generate additional income outside of your primary job. Consider freelance work, consulting, tutoring, or starting a small business. The gig economy offers numerous opportunities to monetize your expertise and talents.

Passive Income and Investment Opportunities

In addition to your primary income, focus on creating passive income streams. money earned with minimal effort or ongoing work can be referred to as Passive income. It can provide a reliable source of income even after you retire.

Explore different passive income opportunities such as rental properties, dividend-paying stocks, peer-to-peer lending, or creating digital products. Each passive income stream requires initial effort and investment, but it can generate continuous income over time.

Optimizing Your Savings Rate

Increasing your income is only one side of the equation. To retire early, you must also optimize your savings rate. Start by closely examining your expenses and identifying areas where you can reduce or eliminate unnecessary spending. Cut back on discretionary expenses and prioritize your financial goals.

Consider implementing the "pay yourself first" principle by automatically allocating a portion of your income towards savings and investments. Set up automatic transfers from your paycheck to your savings or investment accounts. This approach ensures that saving becomes a priority, and you're less likely to spend the money impulsively.

Embrace a frugal lifestyle and practice mindful spending. Differentiate between needs and wants, and question every purchase before making it. Look for ways to save on everyday expenses, such as shopping for discounts, using coupons, or opting for cheaper alternatives. Small savings over time can add up significantly.

Investing Wisely for Long-Term Growth

To make your money work for you, develop a solid investment strategy. Begin by acquiring knowledge on various investment options, including stocks, bonds, mutual funds, or real estate. Understand the associated risks, returns, and diversification benefits of each option.

Consider a long-term investment approach that focuses on growth. Invest in low-cost index funds or exchange-traded funds (ETFs) that track the performance of broad market indexes. These options offer diversification and have historically provided solid returns over time.

Consistently assess and adjust your investment portfolio to ensure that it corresponds with your risk tolerance and financial objectives. Seek the guidance of a financial advisor if needed to create a well-rounded investment strategy.

By maximizing your income through negotiations, side hustles, and passive income streams, and optimizing your savings rate through mindful spending and strategic investments, you'll be well on your way to achieving your early retirement goals.

Remember, consistency and discipline are key. Stay focused on your financial objectives and regularly reassess your progress. With dedication and smart financial choices, you'll be closer to the dream of retiring early and enjoying financial independence.

> *"Early retirement isn't an age; it's a financial state of mind achieved through intentional living and strategic planning."*

4

BUILDING A SOLID FINANCIAL FOUNDATION

In order to achieve early retirement, it's essential to build a solid financial foundation. This chapter will guide you through the steps of organizing your finances, creating an emergency fund, and managing your debt.

Organizing Your Finances

The first step towards a solid financial foundation is to organize your finances. Take the time to gather all your financial documents, including bank statements, investment statements, and bills. Create a system to track your income, expenses, and savings. Utilize spreadsheets or budgeting apps to help you stay organized and monitor your progress.

Next, create a comprehensive budget that outlines your income and expenses. Categorize your expenses into fixed costs (such as rent/mortgage, utilities, and insurance) and variable costs (such as groceries, entertainment, and dining out). This will give you a clear understanding of where your money is going and help you identify areas where you can make adjustments.

Emergency Fund: Your Financial Cushion

An essential cornerstone of a sturdy financial framework is the establishment of an emergency fund. Life's uncertainties bring unforeseen expenses that can throw a wrench into your financial journey. Strive to accumulate a safety net equivalent to three to six months' worth of living expenses in an easily accessible account. This fund serves as a safeguard during unexpected events, offering both peace of mind and financial resilience.

Initiate the construction of your emergency fund by earmarking a portion of your income every month. Make it a top priority and incorporate it into your routine as a regular expense. Explore the option of automating your savings through scheduled transfers from your paycheck to a dedicated savings account. This automated approach ensures a consistent influx of contributions and curbs the inclination to divert funds elsewhere.

Effectively Managing Your Liabilities

Debt poses a significant hurdle on the path to early retirement, necessitating a strategic plan for its management and eventual eradication. Commence by cataloging all debts, encompassing credit card balances, student loans, and any outstanding loans, detailing interest rates and minimum monthly payments for each.

Contemplate the adoption of a debt repayment strategy, such as the snowball or avalanche method. The snowball method directs your focus towards paying off the smallest debt initially, maintaining minimum payments on others. Upon clearing the smallest debt, progress to the next in line, continuing the pattern.

Conversely, the avalanche method prioritizes settling debts with the highest interest rates first. By diligently cultivating an emergency fund and strategically managing your debt, you fortify your financial position, paving the way for a smoother journey towards early retirement.

In addition to your debt repayment plan, look for opportunities to lower your interest rates. Explore options like balance transfers or refinancing to reduce the overall interest you pay. It's also important to avoid taking on new debt while you're working towards early retirement.

Financial Education and Professional Help

Building a solid financial foundation requires knowledge and understanding of personal finance principles. Educate yourself on topics like investing, budgeting, and retirement planning. Read books, listen to podcasts, and follow reputable financial experts to expand your financial literacy.

Consider seeking professional help from a financial advisor who specializes in early retirement planning. They can provide personalized guidance, help you create a tailored financial plan, and offer strategies to optimize your investments and tax planning.

By organizing your finances, building an emergency fund, and managing your debt effectively, you'll establish a strong financial foundation that will support your journey towards early retirement. Stay committed to your financial goals, adapt as needed, and celebrate each milestone along the way. Remember, financial freedom is within your reach with careful planning and disciplined execution.

> *"Financial independence is the cornerstone of the early retirement blueprint, empowering individuals to live life on their terms."*

5

INVESTING FOR LONG-TERM GROWTH

Investing is a critical component of building wealth and achieving early retirement. In this chapter, we will explore the principles of long-term investing, asset allocation, and diversification.

Understanding Long-Term Investing

When it comes to investing for early retirement, it's important to adopt a long-term mindset. Investing is not a get-rich-quick scheme, but rather a strategy that requires patience and discipline. The key is to focus on the long-term growth potential of your investments rather than short-term fluctuations.

Start by setting clear financial goals for your early retirement. Determine the amount of money you'll need to accumulate and the timeline you're aiming for. This will help you establish a target rate of return and guide your investment decisions.

Strategic Asset Distribution: Harmonizing Risk and Reward

The art of asset allocation involves distributing your investment portfolio across diverse asset classes, including stocks, bonds, and cash equivalents. This method aims to strike a balance between risk and return, taking into consideration your individual risk tolerance and investment timeframe.

Historically, stocks have demonstrated the potential for higher returns but accompany heightened volatility. In contrast, bonds present a more stable option with lower returns. Cash equivalents, exemplified by money market funds, contribute liquidity and stability to your portfolio but come with minimal growth potential.

By tactically navigating asset allocation, you sculpt a financial strategy that aligns with your risk preferences and investment horizon, fostering a nuanced equilibrium between potential returns and exposure to risk.

Diversification: Spreading Risk

Diversification is a tactic that entails distributing your investments across various asset classes, industries, and geographic regions.. By diversifying your portfolio, you reduce the risk of significant losses if one investment performs poorly.

Consider investing in a mix of domestic and international stocks, bonds with varying maturities, and different sectors of the economy. This will help protect your portfolio against market fluctuations and potentially enhance your overall returns.

Regular Monitoring and Rebalancing

Investing is not a one-time event. It requires regular monitoring and rebalancing to ensure your portfolio remains aligned with your goals and risk tolerance. Review your investment performance at least annually and make adjustments as needed.

During the rebalancing process, reallocate your investments to maintain your desired asset allocation. For example, if stocks have performed well and now comprise a larger portion of your portfolio than intended, you may need to sell some stocks and invest in other asset classes to restore balance.

Investing for early retirement requires discipline, knowledge, and a long-term perspective. Educate yourself about investment strategies, understand the risks involved, and seek professional advice when needed. Remember, investing is a journey, and staying committed to your plan will increase your chances of achieving your financial goals.

In the next chapter, we will explore the importance of maintaining a healthy work-life balance while striving for early retirement.

"In the early retirement blueprint, every dollar saved is a step closer to freedom from the 9-to-5 grind."

6

BALANCING WORK AND LIFE ON THE PATH TO EARLY RETIREMENT

Striving for early retirement doesn't mean sacrificing your well-being or neglecting other aspects of your life. In this chapter, we will delve into the importance of maintaining a healthy work-life balance while pursuing your financial goals.

Recognizing the Value of Time

As you embark on your journey towards early retirement, it's crucial to recognize the value of time. Time is a limited asset, and it is crucial to utilize it judiciously.. While working towards financial independence, it's essential to strike a balance between your career and personal life.

Evaluate your priorities and determine how you want to spend your time. Identify activities that bring you joy, fulfillment, and contribute to your overall well-being. This can include spending quality time with loved ones, pursuing hobbies, engaging in physical activity, or simply taking time for self-care.

Establishing Limits and Emphasizing Personal Well-being

Sustaining a harmonious work-life equilibrium necessitates the creation of boundaries and a commitment to prioritizing self-care. Define distinct limits between professional and personal spheres, making a conscious effort to uphold them. Steer clear of excessive work demands and refrain from allowing job-related stress to encroach upon your personal time.

Give precedence to self-care by integrating activities that foster your physical, mental, and emotional health into your routine. This may involve regular exercise, mindfulness practices, spending time outdoors, engaging in meditation, or participating in activities that bring joy and relaxation.

Creating a Supportive Environment

Surround yourself with a supportive network of family, friends, and like-minded individuals who understand and share your goals. Connect with others who are also on the path to early retirement, as they can provide valuable guidance, inspiration, and accountability.

Communicate your aspirations and boundaries with your loved ones and colleagues. Share your vision for early retirement and the steps you're taking to achieve it. By involving others in your journey, you'll build a support system that can help you navigate challenges and celebrate milestones.

Continuously Assessing and Adjusting

Consistently evaluate your equilibrium between work and personal life, and make necessary adjustments.. As you progress towards early retirement, your priorities and circumstances may change. Periodically reevaluate your goals, values, and how you're allocating your time and energy.

Consider implementing strategies such as time-blocking or creating a schedule that prioritizes both work and personal activities. This will help you allocate time effectively and prevent one aspect from overshadowing the other.

Remember, the ultimate goal of early retirement is to enjoy a fulfilling and meaningful life. Strive for balance, prioritize self-care, and make conscious choices that align with your values and long-term vision.

In the next chapter, we will explore strategies for maintaining motivation and staying on track during the sometimes-challenging path to early retirement.

"Retiring early is the culmination of aligning your values with your financial goals and having the courage to pursue unconventional paths."

7

STAYING MOTIVATED ON THE PATH TO EARLY RETIREMENT

The journey towards early retirement can be long and challenging. It requires dedication, discipline, and perseverance. In this chapter, we will explore strategies to help you stay motivated and on track towards your goal of early retirement.

1. *Visualize Your Future*: Take the time to envision your ideal retirement lifestyle. Imagine the freedom, flexibility, and fulfillment that early retirement will bring. Create a vision board or write a detailed description of what your life will look like once you achieve financial independence. Visualizing your future can help you stay motivated and remind you of the rewards that await you.

2. *Set Milestones*: Break down your journey towards early retirement into smaller, manageable milestones. Celebrate for each milestone you achieve on your journey. This can be reaching a specific savings target, paying off a significant amount of debt, or reaching a certain investment milestone. Setting and celebrating milestones will provide you with a sense of accomplishment and keep you motivated throughout the process.

3. Find Your Why: Reflect on the reasons why early retirement is important to you. Is it to spend more time with family and loved ones? Pursue your passions and hobbies? Travel the world? Understanding your underlying motivations will help you stay focused and committed when faced with challenges or setbacks.

4. *Surround Yourself with Support:* Connect with like-minded individuals who are also on the path to early retirement. Join online communities, attend meetups or conferences, or even start a mastermind group. Surrounding yourself with people who share your goals and aspirations can provide support, encouragement, and valuable insights. Share your progress, challenges, and successes with your support network, and lean on them for motivation and accountability.

5. *Track Your Progress:* Keep a record of your progress towards early retirement. Track your savings, investment growth, and debt reduction. Seeing your progress visually can be immensely motivating. Use spreadsheets, financial apps, or even a simple pen and paper to track your journey. Celebrate each milestone and use any setbacks or challenges as learning opportunities to improve your strategy.

6. *Continuous Learning:* Educate yourself about personal finance, investment strategies, and retirement planning. The more knowledge you acquire, the more confident and empowered you'll feel. Read books, listen to podcasts, attend workshops, or even consider taking courses on financial literacy and investment management. Continuous learning will not only help you make informed decisions but also keep you engaged and motivated on your path to early retirement.

7. *Practice Self-Care:* Taking care of your physical, mental, and emotional well-being is crucial on the journey towards early retirement. Give precedence to self-care pursuits like exercising, practicing meditation, ensuring sufficient sleep, and maintaining a nutritious diet. Participate in activities that bring you happiness and contribute to recharging your energy. By maintaining a healthy lifestyle, you'll have the energy and resilience to stay motivated and focused on your goals.

Remember, the path to early retirement is not always smooth, and there may be obstacles along the way. Stay committed, stay motivated, and stay focused on the rewards that await you. With determination, persistence, and these strategies in place, you can continue making progress towards your goal of early retirement.

In the next chapter, we will explore strategies for managing unexpected expenses and financial setbacks on your journey to early retirement.

"The early retirement blueprint requires sacrifices today for the freedom to live abundantly tomorrow."

NAVIGATING FINANCIAL SETBACKS ON THE PATH TO EARLY RETIREMENT

While the journey towards early retirement is exciting, it's essential to prepare for unexpected expenses and financial setbacks along the way. In this chapter, we will explore strategies to help you navigate these challenges and stay on track towards your goal.

1. *Emergency Fund:* Building and maintaining an emergency fund is crucial to protect yourself from unexpected expenses. Strive to accumulate a reserve equivalent to three to six months' worth of living expenses in a dedicated and readily accessible account. This fund will act as a safety net and provide you with peace of mind during challenging times.

2. *Risk Management:* Evaluate your insurance coverage to ensure you are adequately protected. This includes health insurance, disability insurance, and homeowner's or renter's insurance. Understand the terms and conditions of your policies and make necessary adjustments to mitigate potential risks.

3. *Flexibility in Spending:* Be prepared to adjust your spending habits and lifestyle if unexpected expenses arise. Adopting a flexible mindset and being willing to make necessary changes will help you navigate financial setbacks without derailing your early retirement plans. Prioritize your needs over wants and focus on long-term financial stability.

4. *Reassess Your Plan:* If faced with a significant financial setback, take the time to reassess your plan and make adjustments as needed. Evaluate your savings rate, investment strategy, and timeline for early retirement. It may be necessary to extend your timeline or increase your savings rate to recover from the setback.

5. *Seek Professional Advice:* Consider consulting with a financial advisor during times of financial uncertainty or setbacks. A professional can provide guidance, help you assess your options, and create a revised plan to get you back on track. Their expertise will be invaluable in navigating complex financial situations.

6. *Maintain a Positive Mindset*: It's natural to feel discouraged or frustrated when faced with financial setbacks. However, maintaining a positive mindset is crucial to overcoming these challenges. Focus on the progress you've made so far and remind yourself of your long-term goals. Use setbacks as opportunities to learn and grow, and stay committed to your vision of early retirement.

7. *Stay Persistent and Resilient:* Financial setbacks are a part of life, but they don't define your journey towards early retirement. Be persistent and resilient even in the face of difficulties. Remember that setbacks are temporary, and with perseverance, you can

overcome them. Stay focused on your long-term goals and continue taking steps towards financial independence.

By being prepared, adaptable, and resilient, you can navigate unexpected expenses and financial setbacks with confidence. Keep your emergency fund well-funded, reassess your plan when needed, and seek professional advice when necessary. With determination and a proactive mindset, you can overcome challenges and stay on track towards your goal of early retirement.

In the next chapter, we will explore strategies for maintaining a healthy work-life balance while pursuing your financial goals.

"True wealth in the context of early retirement isn't just about money; it's about having the autonomy to design a life of purpose and fulfillment."

CULTIVATING MINDFULNESS AND WELL-BEING ON THE PATH TO EARLY RETIREMENT

As you strive for early retirement, it's important to prioritize your well-being and cultivate mindfulness along the way. In this chapter, we will explore strategies to help you maintain a healthy mind and body, fostering a sense of overall well-being on the path to early retirement.

1. ***Practice Mindfulness:*** Incorporate mindfulness practices into your daily routine. Mindfulness entails immersing yourself entirely in the present moment, attentively observing your thoughts, emotions, and sensations without passing judgment.. Engage in activities such as meditation, deep breathing exercises, or mindful walking to cultivate a sense of calm and awareness. Mindfulness can help reduce stress, increase focus, and enhance overall mental well-being.

2. ***Give Importance to Personal Well-being:*** Ensure that self-care becomes an essential and non-negotiable aspect of your daily routine. Take time to engage in activities that promote relaxation, rejuvenation, and self-reflection. This can include reading, taking

baths, practicing yoga, or journaling. Prioritizing self-care will help you recharge and maintain a healthy work-life balance.

3. *Nurture Relationships:* Cultivate meaningful connections with loved ones and friends. Dedicate time to nurture your relationships, whether it's through quality time spent together, heartfelt conversations, or acts of kindness. Strong social connections contribute to overall well-being and can provide support and joy on your journey towards early retirement.

4. *Engage in Physical Activity:* Regular exercise is essential for both physical and mental well-being. Find physical activities that you enjoy, whether it's hiking, dancing, cycling, or practicing yoga. Engaging in regular exercise releases endorphins, reduces stress, and boosts energy levels, enabling you to stay focused and motivated on your path to early retirement.

5. *Practice Gratitude:* Cultivate a gratitude practice by regularly expressing appreciation for the positive aspects of your life. Achieve this by engaging in journaling, establishing a gratitude jar, or dedicating a few moments each day to reflect on the things you are thankful for.. Gratitude promotes a positive mindset, increases resilience, and enhances overall well-being.

6. *Disconnect from Technology:* In today's digital age, it's important to create boundaries with technology. Allocate specific periods to detach from screens and participate in activities that foster relaxation and mindfulness. This can include reading a book, going for a walk in nature, or engaging in creative hobbies. Disconnecting from technology allows you to recharge and be present in the moment.

7. *Seek Support:* Reach out for support when needed. If you find yourself feeling overwhelmed or struggling with your journey towards early retirement, don't hesitate to seek professional help or join support groups. Therapists, financial advisors, and like-minded individuals can provide guidance, perspective, and encouragement.

By prioritizing mindfulness and well-being, you'll be better equipped to navigate the challenges and enjoy the rewards of early retirement. Incorporate mindfulness practices, prioritize self-care, nurture relationships, engage in physical activity, practice gratitude, disconnect from technology, and seek support when needed. Remember, your well-being is just as important as your financial goals on this journey towards early retirement.

In the next chapter, we will delve into strategies for maintaining motivation and overcoming obstacles on the path to early retirement.

> *"In the early retirement blueprint, time is your most valuable asset, and every decision should be made with its preservation in mind."*

10

OVERCOMING OBSTACLES AND MAINTAINING MOTIVATION ON THE PATH TO EARLY RETIREMENT

As you pursue early retirement, you will inevitably encounter obstacles and face moments when your motivation wavers. In this chapter, we will explore strategies to help you overcome these challenges and maintain your drive towards financial independence.

1. *Identify Potential Obstacles:* Take the time to identify potential obstacles that may arise on your path to early retirement. This could include unexpected expenses, market fluctuations, or changes in personal circumstances. By anticipating and acknowledging these challenges, you can develop proactive strategies to overcome them.

2. *Create a Contingency Plan:* Develop a contingency plan for potential obstacles. Consider different scenarios and devise alternative strategies to stay on track. This could involve adjusting your savings rate, diversifying your investments, or exploring additional income streams. Having a plan in place will provide you with a sense of security and confidence.

3. *Stay Flexible and Adaptive:* Embrace flexibility and adaptability as you encounter obstacles. Recognize that setbacks are a natural part of any journey and that adjustments may be needed along the way. Embracing change and being open to new strategies will help you navigate challenges and maintain momentum towards your goal.

4. *Break Down Goals into Manageable Steps:* Sometimes, the path to early retirement can feel overwhelming. To combat this, break down your larger goal into smaller, manageable steps. Set for yourself milestones and celebrate each one you achieve. This approach not only provides a sense of accomplishment but also helps you stay motivated and focused on the progress you're making.

5. *Find Inspiration and Accountability:* Surround yourself with sources of inspiration and accountability. Seek out stories of individuals who have achieved early retirement and learn from their experiences. Engage with online communities, attend workshops or conferences, or even consider finding an accountability partner. Having a support system and access to resources can help you stay motivated during challenging times.

6. *Revisit Your Reasons:* Regularly remind yourself of the reasons why early retirement is important to you. Reflect on the lifestyle you envision and the freedom it will provide. Reconnecting with your underlying motivations will reignite your passion and help you persevere when faced with obstacles.

7. *Practice Self-Reflection:* Take time for self-reflection and introspection. Assess your progress, evaluate your strategies, and identify areas for improvement. Regular self-reflection allows you

to course-correct, learn from past experiences, and continuously refine your approach towards early retirement.

8. *Celebrate Milestones:* Celebrate your achievements along the way. Each milestone, no matter how small, is a step forward towards your ultimate goal. Acknowledge and treat yourself for your diligent efforts and commitment. It's important to acknowledge and appreciate your progress as you navigate the challenges of early retirement.

Remember, the journey to early retirement is not always smooth, but with determination, adaptability, and a positive mindset, you can overcome obstacles and maintain your motivation. Identify potential challenges, create contingency plans, stay flexible, break down goals, find inspiration, revisit your reasons, practice self-reflection, and celebrate milestones. By doing so, you'll continue making progress towards the financial independence you desire.

In the next chapter, we will explore strategies for managing time effectively and maintaining a healthy work-life balance as you pursue early retirement.

> *"The early retirement blueprint is a journey of self-discovery, where your values shape your financial decisions and your financial decisions shape your future."*

11

EFFECTIVE TIME MANAGEMENT AND WORK-LIFE BALANCE ON THE PATH TO EARLY RETIREMENT

As you work towards early retirement, managing your time effectively and maintaining a healthy work-life balance becomes crucial. In this chapter, we will explore strategies to help you optimize your time, prioritize your activities, and create a fulfilling balance between work and personal life.

1. ***Establish Clear Objectives and Priorities:*** Commence by outlining your goals and priorities. What do you want to achieve in your work, personal life, and on the path to early retirement? By clarifying your objectives, you can focus your time and energy on activities that align with your long-term vision.

2. ***Create a Schedule and Stick to It:*** Develop a schedule that reflects your priorities and goals. Allocate specific time blocks for work, personal activities, and relaxation. Be disciplined and stick to your schedule as much as possible, avoiding distractions and unnecessary time-wasting activities.

3. *Delegate and Outsource:* Recognize that you don't have to do everything by yourself. Delegate tasks at work and consider outsourcing certain responsibilities in your personal life. Hiring a virtual assistant, house cleaner, or lawn care service can free up valuable time and energy for more important endeavors.

4. *Practice Effective Time Blocking:* Use time blocking techniques to maximize productivity. Dedicate specific blocks of time to focus on important tasks or projects, minimizing interruptions and distractions. This approach allows you to work efficiently and make progress towards your goals.

5. *Learn to Say No:* It's essential to set boundaries and learn to say no to activities or commitments that don't align with your priorities. Prioritize your time and energy for activities that contribute to your long-term goals and well-being. Saying no allows you to maintain focus and avoid unnecessary distractions.

6. *Embrace Work-Life Integration:* Instead of striving for a strict separation between work and personal life, aim for work-life integration. Find ways to incorporate activities that bring you joy and relaxation into your workday. Take breaks to exercise, meditate, or engage in hobbies that rejuvenate your mind and body.

7. *Practice Self-Care:* Make self-care a priority in your daily routine. Engage in activities that promote relaxation, mental well-being, and physical health. This can include exercise, meditation, spending time in nature, or pursuing creative hobbies. Taking care of yourself allows you to show up more fully in both work and personal life.

8. *Foster Supportive Relationships:* Surround yourself with supportive individuals who understand and respect your goals. Cultivate relationships with like-minded individuals who can provide encouragement, accountability, and understanding. Having a strong support system can help you navigate the challenges of balancing work and personal life on the path to early retirement.

9. *Regularly Assess and Adjust:* Periodically assess how you are managing your time and work-life balance. Contemplate what is functioning effectively and identify areas requiring modification. Be willing to make changes as needed to ensure that you are prioritizing your well-being and progress towards early retirement.

By implementing these strategies, you can effectively manage your time, prioritize your activities, and create a fulfilling work-life balance on your journey towards early retirement.

Set clear goals, create a schedule, delegate and outsource when necessary, practice effective time blocking, learn to say no, embrace work-life integration, practice self-care, foster supportive relationships, and regularly assess and adjust. With these practices in place, you'll be better equipped to maintain a healthy balance and make progress towards your financial independence.

In the next chapter, we will explore strategies for maintaining motivation and staying focused as you approach the final stages of your journey towards early retirement.

"Retiring early isn't an escape from work but a transition to meaningful pursuits that align with your passions and values."

12

SUSTAINING MOTIVATION AND FOCUS IN THE FINAL STAGES OF EARLY RETIREMENT JOURNEY

As you approach the final stages of your journey towards early retirement, it's crucial to sustain your motivation and stay focused on your goals. In this chapter, we will explore strategies to help you navigate the final stretch, overcome any potential roadblocks, and maintain your determination.

1. *Visualize Your Ideal Retirement:* Keep your vision of early retirement vivid and alive in your mind. Take the time to visualize what your ideal retirement looks like and how it will feel to achieve financial independence. This visualization can serve as a powerful motivator during challenging times and help you stay focused on your end goal.

2. *Break Down Your Remaining Milestones:* Analyze the remaining milestones and tasks to be accomplished before reaching early retirement. Break them down into smaller, manageable steps. This approach allows you to track your progress and celebrate your achievements along the way, reinforcing your motivation.

3. *Review and Update Your Financial Plan:* Regularly review and update your financial plan as you approach the final stages of your journey. Take into account any changes in your income, expenses, or investment strategies. This review will help you stay on track and ensure that your plan remains aligned with your goals.

4. *Stay Informed and Engaged:* Stay informed about personal finance and retirement-related topics. Continuously educate yourself about investment strategies, tax implications, and retirement planning. Engaging with relevant information and resources will help you make informed decisions and maintain your motivation.

5. *Seek Inspiration from Others:* Surround yourself with stories of individuals who have successfully achieved early retirement. Seek out books, blogs, podcasts, or communities where you can find inspiration and learn from their experiences. Hearing about others' journeys can reignite your motivation and provide valuable insights.

6. *Stay Flexible and Adapt to Changing Circumstances:* Remain flexible and adaptable as you approach the final stages of your early retirement journey. Life is unpredictable, and circumstances may change. Be prepared to adjust your plans and strategies accordingly, while staying focused on your ultimate goal.

7. *Celebrate Your Progress:* Take the time to celebrate your progress and achievements along the way. Celebrating milestones, no matter how small, will boost your morale and reinforce your determination to reach early retirement. Treat yourself to small rewards or engage in activities that bring you joy as you move closer to your goal.

8. *Connect with Like-Minded Individuals:* Surround yourself with like-minded individuals who share your goals and aspirations. Engage in communities, attend networking events, or join online forums where you can connect with others on a similar journey. Sharing experiences, challenges, and successes with others will provide invaluable support and motivation.

9. *Practice Self-Care and Stress Management:* Prioritize self-care and stress management as you approach the final stages of your journey. Take care of your physical and mental well-being, ensuring that you have the energy and resilience to stay focused. Engage in activities that help you relax, recharge, and maintain a healthy balance.

10. *Stay Grateful and Reflect on Your Progress:* Cultivate an attitude of gratitude and regularly reflect on how far you've come. Acknowledge the efforts and sacrifices you've made to reach this point. Express gratitude for the opportunities and resources that have supported you on your journey. This practice will help you stay positive and motivated.

By implementing these strategies, you can sustain your motivation and stay focused as you approach the final stages of your early retirement journey. Visualize your ideal retirement, break down your remaining milestones, review and update your financial plan, stay informed and engaged, seek inspiration, stay flexible, celebrate your progress, connect with like-minded individuals, practice self-care, and stay grateful for your achievements.

With these practices in place, you'll be well-equipped to overcome challenges and successfully reach early retirement.

In the next chapter, we will explore strategies for transitioning into early retirement and navigating the exciting new chapter of your life.

> *"The early retirement blueprint is about optimizing your life for happiness, fulfillment, and freedom, rather than blindly chasing societal norms."*

13

TRANSITIONING INTO EARLY RETIREMENT – EMBRACING A NEW CHAPTER

Congratulations! You've reached the exciting milestone of early retirement. Now, it's time to navigate the transition and embrace this new chapter of your life. In this chapter, we will explore strategies to help you make a smooth and fulfilling transition into early retirement.

1. *Reflect on Your Retirement Vision:* Take some time to reflect on the retirement vision you had during your journey. Assess if it aligns with your current desires and aspirations. This reflection will help you gain clarity on how you want to shape your retirement and set meaningful goals for this new phase.

2. *Establish a New Routine:* Although retirement is often associated with freedom from routines, having a new structure can provide a sense of purpose and fulfillment. Create a daily or weekly routine that includes activities you enjoy, such as pursuing hobbies, engaging in volunteer work, or learning new skills. A routine will

give you a sense of direction and help you make the most of your retirement years.

3. **Stay Engaged and Active:** Retirement doesn't mean disengagement from the world. Stay active and involved in your community or pursue activities that keep you mentally and physically stimulated. Join clubs, organizations, or groups that align with your interests and values. This engagement will provide a sense of belonging and fulfillment in your retired life.

4. **Manage Your Finances:** Even though you've achieved early retirement, it's essential to continue managing your finances wisely. Review your financial plan regularly, monitor your expenses, and ensure that your retirement savings are aligned with your desired lifestyle. Being financially aware will give you peace of mind and allow you to enjoy retirement without financial worries.

5. **Prioritize Health and Wellness:** Make your well-being a top priority in retirement. Focus on maintaining a healthy lifestyle through regular exercise, nutritious eating, and regular check-ups. Allocate time for self-care activities that enhance relaxation, alleviate stress, and contribute to mental well-being.. A healthy body and mind will enable you to fully enjoy your retirement years.

6. **Set New Goals and Pursue Passions:** Retirement offers a chance to explore new passions and interests. Set new goals for yourself, whether it's learning a musical instrument, writing a book, traveling to new destinations, or starting a new business venture. Pursuing these passions will bring excitement and fulfillment to your retired life.

7. *Foster Relationships and Connections:* Invest time and effort in nurturing relationships with loved ones and building new connections. Spend quality time with family and friends, plan gatherings or trips together, and engage in meaningful conversations. Building and maintaining strong relationships will enhance your retired life's joy and sense of belonging.

8. *Embrace Leisure and Relaxation:* Take the opportunity to embrace leisure and relaxation in your retirement. Engage in activities that bring you joy, such as reading, gardening, painting, or exploring nature. Allow yourself to slow down and savor the simple pleasures of life. Embracing leisure will help you find balance and contentment in your retired years.

9. *Continuously Learn and Grow:* Retirement doesn't mean the end of personal growth and learning. Engage in lifelong learning by taking courses, attending workshops, or pursuing new certifications. Constantly challenging yourself intellectually will keep your mind sharp and open doors to new possibilities in retirement.

10. *Stay Flexible and Embrace Change:* Be open to change and adapt to new circumstances in retirement. Life is unpredictable, and embracing flexibility will allow you to navigate any unexpected events or opportunities that come your way. Embracing change will keep your retirement dynamic and exciting.

By implementing these strategies, you can make a smooth transition into early retirement and embrace this new chapter of your life. Reflect on your retirement vision, establish a new routine, stay engaged and active, manage your finances, prioritize health and wellness, set new goals, foster relationships, embrace leisure, continuously learn and grow, and stay flexible. With these practices in place, you'll be well-prepared to enjoy a fulfilling and purposeful retirement.

In the final chapter, we will conclude our journey by reflecting on your achievements, celebrating your success, and offering final words of wisdom as you embark on this incredible new phase of your life.

"In the early retirement blueprint, every dollar saved and invested is a seed planted for a future of abundance and opportunity."

14

REFLECTING ON YOUR ACHIEVEMENTS AND CELEBRATING SUCCESS

As you near the end of this book and your journey towards early retirement, it's important to take the time to reflect on your achievements and celebrate your success. In this chapter, we will guide you through a process of reflection and offer ways to commemorate this significant milestone.

1. *Journal Your Journey:* Take out your journal and reflect on the entire process of your early retirement journey. Write about the challenges you faced, the lessons you learned, and the growth you experienced along the way. Capture your emotions, thoughts, and significant moments. This journal will serve as a precious record of your achievement and a source of inspiration for others.

2. *Express Gratitude:* Gratitude is a powerful practice that can bring immense joy and fulfillment. Take a moment to express gratitude for the opportunities, resources, and support that allowed you to reach early retirement. Consider writing thank-you notes or expressing your appreciation to the people who played a significant

role in your journey. Gratitude will cultivate a positive mindset and deepen your sense of fulfillment.

3. ***Celebrate Milestones:*** Celebrate the milestones you achieved throughout your early retirement journey. Whether it's reaching a specific savings goal, paying off debt, or making significant investment decisions, each milestone is worth acknowledging. Plan a small celebration or treat yourself to something special to commemorate your accomplishments. Celebrating milestones will reinforce your confidence and motivation.

4. ***Share Your Story:*** Consider sharing your early retirement story with others. Whether it's through writing a blog post, giving a presentation, or writing an article, sharing your journey can inspire and motivate others who are on a similar path. Your story can provide valuable insights and guidance, making a positive impact on others' lives.

5. ***Engage in Meaningful Reflection:*** Engage in meaningful reflection by asking yourself thought-provoking questions. What did you learn about yourself during this journey? How have your priorities and values evolved? What are you most proud of achieving? Reflecting on these questions will help you gain valuable insights and deepen your understanding of the transformative power of your early retirement journey.

6. ***Create a Memory Box:*** Assemble a memory box filled with mementos from your early retirement journey. Collect photographs, letters, or small objects that symbolize significant moments or milestones. This memory box will serve as a tangible reminder of

your achievements, and you can revisit it whenever you want to reminisce about this remarkable time in your life.

7. ***Plan a Meaningful Trip:*** Consider planning a meaningful trip to celebrate your early retirement. Choose a destination that holds significance for you or that you've always wanted to visit. This trip will serve as a memorable way to mark the end of one chapter and the beginning of another. It will also provide an opportunity for relaxation, reflection, and rejuvenation.

8. ***Pay It Forward:*** Use your early retirement as an opportunity to give back and make a positive impact in your community or the world. Volunteer for causes that resonate with you, donate to organizations you care about, or mentor others who are on a similar journey. Paying it forward will not only benefit others but also bring a sense of fulfillment and purpose to your retired life.

9. ***Engage in New Pursuits:*** Embrace the freedom of early retirement by exploring new passions and pursuits. Take up hobbies, learn new skills, or engage in activities that bring you joy and fulfillment. This phase of your life offers endless possibilities, and embracing new pursuits will keep your life vibrant and exciting.

10. ***Embrace the Journey Ahead:*** As you reflect on your achievements and celebrate your success, embrace the journey that lies ahead in your early retirement. Embrace the endless possibilities, the freedom to pursue your passions, and the opportunity to live life on your own terms. Embrace the joy, fulfillment, and purpose that retirement can bring.

Congratulations on achieving this noteworthy milestone in your life. Reflect on your journey, express gratitude, celebrate milestones, share your story, engage in meaningful reflection, create a memory box, plan a meaningful trip, pay it forward, engage in new pursuits, and embrace the journey ahead.

Your early retirement is a testament to your hard work, determination, and vision. May this next chapter of your life be filled with joy, fulfillment, and endless possibilities.

In the final chapter, we will conclude our book by offering final words of wisdom and encouragement as you embark on this incredible new phase of your life.

"Achieving financial independence and retiring early requires a willingness to challenge conventional wisdom and forge your own path."

15

EMBRACING THE NEXT CHAPTER - FINAL WORDS OF WISDOM

As we come to the end of this book, it's time to offer you some final words of wisdom and encouragement as you embark on this incredible new phase of your life. Early retirement is a remarkable achievement, and you should be proud of the hard work and dedication that brought you here. Now, let's take a moment to reflect and gather some valuable insights for the road ahead.

1. ***Embrace Change and Adaptability:*** Early retirement is a significant transition, and it's essential to embrace change and cultivate your adaptability skills. Life will continue to evolve, presenting you with new opportunities and challenges. By maintaining an open mind and being willing to adapt, you'll be better equipped to navigate the twists and turns that may come your way.

2. ***Continuously Learn and Grow:*** Retirement doesn't mean the end of personal and intellectual growth. In fact, it's the perfect time to explore new interests, learn new skills, and expand your knowledge. Engage in lifelong learning, whether through formal education, online courses, or self-study. Embrace curiosity and the pursuit of knowledge to keep your mind sharp and your retirement fulfilling.

3. *Cultivate a Healthy Work-Life Balance:* While retirement offers freedom from traditional work obligations, it's still crucial to maintain a healthy work-life balance. Find meaningful ways to stay engaged and contribute to your community or pursue personal projects that bring you joy. Strike a balance between rest, relaxation, and pursuing activities that give you a sense of purpose and fulfillment.

4. *Prioritize Your Well-Being:* Your physical, mental, and emotional well-being should always be a top priority. Take care of yourself by engaging in regular exercise, practicing mindfulness or meditation, and nurturing your relationships. Seek support when needed, whether from loved ones or professionals, to ensure you maintain a healthy and balanced lifestyle.

5. *Stay Connected:* One of the most valuable aspects of retirement is the opportunity to deepen your connections with loved ones and build new relationships. Take the time to nurture your relationships and stay connected with family, friends, and your community. Engage in meaningful conversations, create shared experiences, and cherish the bonds that enrich your retired life.

6. *Embrace a Sense of Purpose:* Retirement offers the chance to redefine your sense of purpose and find fulfillment in new ways. Explore activities, causes, or ventures that align with your values and passions. Engage in volunteer work, mentor others, or pursue projects that make a positive impact. Embracing a sense of purpose will bring a deeper meaning to your retired life.

7. *Be Mindful of Your Finances:* Although you've prepared for early retirement, it's crucial to remain mindful of your financial

situation. Continuously review your budget, monitor your investments, and seek professional advice when needed. Being proactive and responsible with your finances will provide the security and peace of mind to fully enjoy your retirement years.

8. *Embrace the Joy of Simple Pleasures:* In the hustle and bustle of life, it's easy to overlook the simple pleasures that bring us joy. Take the time to savor the small moments – a beautiful sunset, a warm cup of coffee, or a leisurely walk in nature. Embrace the joy of simple pleasures and cultivate gratitude for the beauty that surrounds you.

9. *Stay Curious and Adventurous:* Retirement is the perfect time to indulge your curiosity and embrace adventure. Try new experiences, explore different cultures, and step out of your comfort zone. Travel to new destinations, take up a new hobby, or challenge yourself to learn something outside of your expertise. Staying curious and adventurous will keep your retirement years exciting and fulfilling.

10. *Remember to Relax and Enjoy:* Lastly, remember to relax and enjoy this chapter of your life. You've worked hard to reach early retirement, and now it's time to reap the rewards. Embrace the freedom, the flexibility, and the joy that retirement brings. Allow yourself to slow down, find contentment in the present moment, and fully appreciate the incredible journey you've embarked upon.

As you move forward into this next chapter, remember to embrace change, continue learning and growing, prioritize your well-being, stay connected, find purpose, be mindful of your finances, savor the simple pleasures, stay curious and adventurous, and above all, relax and enjoy this remarkable phase of your life.

Congratulations once again on reaching early retirement. May this new chapter be filled with fulfillment, joy, and endless possibilities. Cheers to a life well-lived and a future brimming with excitement and adventure!

ABOUT THE AUTHOR

Jeffrey Feron is a seasoned business consultant with a proven track record of helping numerous organizations achieve their goals and startups establish a strong foundation.

With years of experience in the business world, Jeffrey has become a trusted advisor in the field of entrepreneurship and corporate strategy.

As a business consultant, Jeffrey specializes in providing tailored solutions to organizations seeking growth, efficiency, and innovation. He has an exceptional ability to analyze complex business challenges, identify opportunities, and develop practical strategies that drive success.

His deep understanding of market dynamics, financial management, and industry trends has consistently delivered measurable results for his clients.

One of Jeffrey's standout skills is his expertise in setting up businesses. He has guided countless entrepreneurs through the intricate process of launching their ventures, from initial concept to operational success.

His knowledge spans various industries, making him a versatile resource for anyone looking to embark on their entrepreneurial journey.

Jeffrey Feron is not just a consultant; he's a mentor, motivator, and problem solver. He's known for his dedication to his client's success and his commitment to fostering a culture of innovation and growth.

JEFFREY FERON

Author

Meknatureconcept@gmail.com.

Thank you for choosing this book, if you feel this book is valuable, kindly consider leaving us a review on Amazon. Your feedback is critical to me and others looking for help related to the same book.

www.ingramcontent.com/pod-product-compliance
Lightning Source LLC
Chambersburg PA
CBHW071102290526
45795CB00004B/1620